My First Acrostic

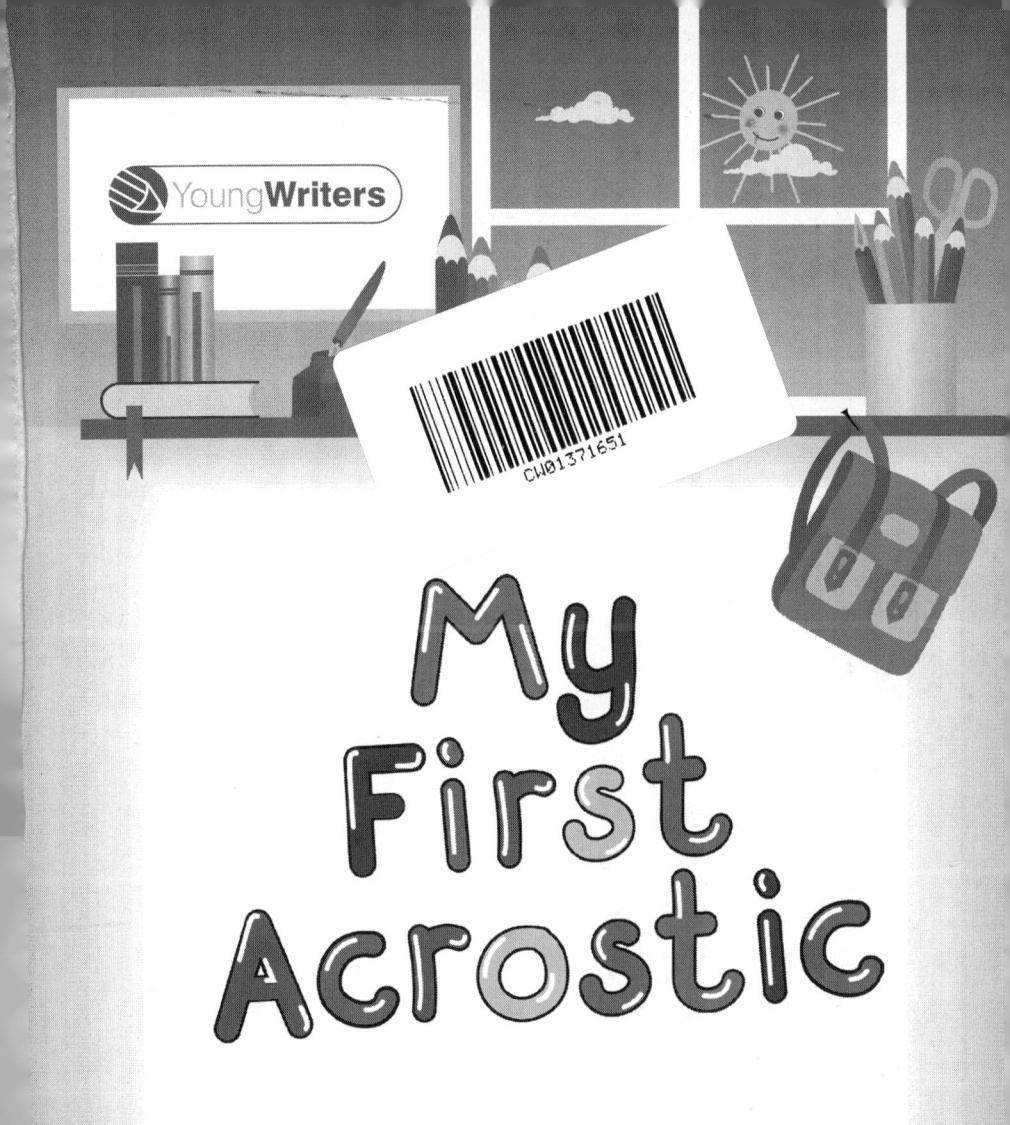

Eastern England

Edited by Lisa Adlam

First published in Great Britain in 2009 by:

YoungWriters

Young Writers
Remus House
Coltsfoot Drive
Peterborough
PE2 9JX
Telephone: 01733 890066
Website: www.youngwriters.co.uk

All Rights Reserved
© Copyright Contributors 2009
SB ISBN 978-1-84924-425-1

Foreword

The 'My First Acrostic' collection was developed by Young Writers specifically for Key Stage 1 children. The poetic form is simple, fun and gives the young poet a guideline to shape their ideas, yet at the same time leaves room for their imagination and creativity to begin to blossom.

Due to the young age of the entrants we have enjoyed rewarding their effort by including as many of the poems as possible. Our hope is that seeing their work in print will encourage the children to grow and develop their writing skills to become our poets of tomorrow.

Young Writers has been publishing children's poetry for over 19 years. Our aim is to nurture creativity in our children and young adults, to give them an interest in poetry and an outlet to express themselves. This latest collection will act as a milestone for the young poets and one that will be enjoyable to revisit again and again.

Contents

All Souls' CE Primary School, Folkestone
Mia Davies (7) 1
Natalie Chwalibogowski (6) 2
Liam Hearnden 3
Suchita Tamang (7) 4
Summer Maguire (5) 5
India Burchell (6) 6
Joshua Pullen (7) 7
Jake Hardie (7) 8
Bethany Lawrence (7) 9
Lewis Hammerton (6) 10
Kayleigh Gladman (7) 11
James Medlen (7) 12
Charlotte Guilbert-Greene 13
Flo-Ellen Britcliffe (6) 14
Kye Johnson 15
Betty Appleton (6) 16
Katie Angus (5) 17
Hangchhu Rai (7) 18
Ashiph Rai (7) 19
Jade McClure (7) 20
Star Nicole Foss (7) 21

Broad Oak Community Primary School, Heathfield
Erin Johnson (7) 22
Mia Terry (6) 23
Zoe Thompson (7) 24
James French (7) 25
Lara Hands (7) 26
Ewan Hazeltine (7) 27
Ben Woodthorpe (7) 28
Jessica Porter (7) 29
Hannah Mepham (7) 30
Kieran Hands (7) 31

Copford CE Primary School, Colchester
Callum Dobson (6) 32
Daisy Norton (7) 33
Mitcham Brand (7) 34
Lilly Hanson (7) 35

Alice Gladwell (7) 36
Rosie Fulford (7) 37
Harriet Chamberlaine (7) 38

Firle CE Primary School, Lewes
Mia Brimilcombe-Cowie (7) 39
David Cooper (7) 40
Madison Piper (6) 41
James Pratley (6) 42
Nathan Lewis (6) 43
Izzy Abey (6) 44
Ava Brimilcombe-Cowie (7) 45
Robert Pratley (6) 46
Luke Freeman (7) 47

Kettlefields Primary School, Newmarket
Jessica Whitehall (7) 48
Stephanie Warr (7) 49
Charlie Nicholas (6) 50
Amy Sellers (7) 51
George O'Shea (7) 52
Milla Jarman-Howe (6) 53
James Dracup (6) 54

Leybourne CE Primary School, West Malling
Ellie Savidge (6) 55
Freddie Francis (6) 56
Philip Coussey (7) 57
Rhiannon Russell (7) 58
Nathan Fox (6) 59
Molly Booker (6) 60
Victoria Fleming (7) 61
Michael Middleton (7) 62
Jack Daniel (7) 63
India Fricker (6) 64
Hannah Collier (6) 65
Ben Young (6) 66
Samuel Dascalescu (7) 67
Alex Kitchener (7) 68
Kiran Henry (6) 69
Nicole Egen (6) 70
Amy Mitchell (6) 71

Jack Whybrow (6) 72
Oliver Temp (6) 73
Jarvis Spratt (6) 74

Little Snoring Primary School, Fakenham
Phoebe Margetson (6) 75
Liberty Cann (6) 76
Milly Eckett (5) 77
Abigail Cator (6) 78
Kyle Williamson (6) 79
Alexander Thomas (7) 80
Kyle Taylor (7) 81
Gwendolen Otte (6) 82
Daniel Ellis-Flinders (7) 83
Harriet Borley (5) 84
Cazy-Rose Flinders (6) 85
Sophie Grinnell (6) 86

Meridan Primary School, Comberton
James Goodchild (6) 87
Phoebe Stearn (6) 88
Liam Cox (6) 89
Jack Jacklin (7) 90
Mia Hoover-Harrison (6) 91
Callan Chambers (5) 92
Michael Wilkinson (6) 93
Phoebe Cornell (7) 94
Yasmin Girling (5) 95
Lauren Davy (6) 96
Madeleine McNiven (6) 97
Mae Bicheno (5) 98
Jacob Sewell (6) 99
Cara Chivers (6) 100
Katie Hartwright (6) 101
Rosanna Poll (6) 102
Oliver Payne (7) 103
Chelsie Alderman (7) 104
Holly Jones (6) 105
Ellen Gourley (6) 106
Leanora O'Mullane (7) 107
Alice Heydinger (7) 108
Sam Collison (7) 109
Delilah Halpin (7) 110
Henry Legood (7) 111
Keenan Christ (7) 112

Alice O'Connell (7) 113
Lucy Carlton (7) 114
Rebecca Allard (6) 115

Nightingale First School, Taverham
Jack Street 116
Hannah Morris-Jones (6) 117
Max Kelly (6) 118
Lilli Forster (5) 119
Jessica Williams 120
Ellen De-Abreu (6) 121
Lauren Mason (6) 122
Jamie Fox (5) 123
Ellie Vicary (5) 124
Macy Guyton (5) 125
Molly McCarthy (5) 126
James Nottingham (6) 127
Jordan Barton (6) 128
Adam Cann (6) 129
Joshua Rendlesome (6) 130
Alana Boyd (6) 131
Lucy Nudds (6) 132
Ebony Leggett (5) 133
Yasmine Lowe (5) 134

Rainham Village Primary School, Rainham
Lewis Ricketts (6) 135
Paige Blackmore (7) 136
Mollie Fell (7) 137
Lakhan Sunder 138
Rianna Theresa Kelly 139
Jamie Godson (7) 140
Niha Raju 141
Fidel Joseph 142
Stephen Crews (7) 143
Rhys Rose (7) 144
Connor Clifford (7) 145
Aminatu Belo-Osagie (6) 146
Shantae Marson 147
Joshua Alaka (7) 148
Dilanas Bidva (6) 149
Julia Muja 150
Katie Reid (5) 151
Camron Brown (6) 152
Coral Finch 153
Ellie Smith 154

Lucy Norman (5) 155
Max Patrick 156
Ciaran Robinson (5) 157
Kadi Bayliss (5) 158
Esther Showeminio (6) 159
Lilian Phillips (5) 160
Katie Fuller (6) 161
Fricis Cirulis (6) 162
Dylan Phillips (6) 163
Demi Daniel (6) 164
Dillon Edwards (5) 165
Gabrielle Hartman (6) 166
Peter Wilson (6) 167

St Faith's School, Cambridge
Holly Todd (6) 168
Sophie Hart (7) 169
William Best (7) 170
Alfie Godsal (7) 171
Hugo Fung (6) 172
Emily Townsend (7) 173
Lara Iqbal Gilling (7) 174
Rocco Benedetto Mozo (7) 175
Molly Punshon (6) 176
Gavin Watt (6) 177

Sproughton Primary School, Ipswich
Edward Ruff (7) 178
Daisy Brosnan (5) 179
Abigail Thomas (5) 180
Adam Hardy (7) 181
Ben Marriott-Gregg (7) 182
Ellisa Kingham (7) 183
Mackenzie Cobb (7) 184
Matthew Earey (7) 185

Whitton CP School, Ipswich
Ryan Hard (5) 186
Aimee Emmerson (6) 187
Amy Perkins (5) 188
Damla Ayran (5) 189
Freddie Acott (6) 190
Unique Smith (6) 191

The Poems

My First Acrostic - Eastern England

Mia Davies

M arvellous
I nteresting
A dorable

D elicate
A rty
V ery nice
I ncredible
E ver so funny
S o sweet.

Mia Davies (7)
All Souls' CE Primary School, Folkestone

Natalie

- **N** ice
- **A** girl
- **T** idy
- **A** marvellous girl
- **L** ight skin
- **I** nteresting
- **E** xcellent.

Natalie Chwalibogowski (6)
All Souls' CE Primary School, Folkestone

My First Acrostic - Eastern England

Liam

L ovely
I nteresting
A cool boy
M agic.

Liam Hearnden
All Souls' CE Primary School, Folkestone

Suchita

S weet
U nique
C uddly
H appy
I CT
T all
A lways.

Suchita Tamang (7)
All Souls' CE Primary School, Folkestone

My First Acrostic - Eastern England

Summer

S he is beautiful
U nique
M agic
M arvellous
E xcellent
R eally good.

Summer Maguire (5)
All Souls' CE Primary School, Folkestone

India

I nteresting
N ice
D angerous
I ncredible
A nd careful.

India Burchell (6)
All Souls' CE Primary School, Folkestone

My First Acrostic - Eastern England

Joshua

J umpy
O h fantastic
S miley
H elpful
U seful
A lways friendly.

Joshua Pullen (7)
All Souls' CE Primary School, Folkestone

Jake

J umpy
A lways good
K ind
E xcellent.

Jake Hardie (7)
All Souls' CE Primary School, Folkestone

My First Acrostic - Eastern England

Bethany Lawrence

B eautiful hair
E ver so funny
T hankful
H appy
A dorable
N early short hair
Y oung big girl

L ovely
A big pretty girl
W riting girl
R eally popular
E arly riser
N ice
C aring and cuddly
E ver so kind.

Bethany Lawrence (7)
All Souls' CE Primary School, Folkestone

Lewis

L ovely eyes
E xcellent at maths
W ise
I tch in my jumper
S uper at computers.

Lewis Hammerton (6)
All Souls' CE Primary School, Folkestone

My First Acrostic - Eastern England

Kayleigh

K ind
A beautiful girl
Y ellow hair
L ovely
E ver so nice
I nteresting
G ood girl
H elpful.

Kayleigh Gladman (7)
All Souls' CE Primary School, Folkestone

James

J ames is a lovely boy
A special boy
M arvellous
E xcellent
S hort hair.

James Medlen (7)
All Souls' CE Primary School, Folkestone

My First Acrostic - Eastern England

Charlotte

C lever
H elpful
A lways happy
R uns fast
L ovely clothes
O h!
T idy
T all
E xcellent.

Charlotte Guilbert-Greene
All Souls' CE Primary School, Folkestone

Flo-Ellen

F unny
L ikeable
O h fantastic
E xcellent
-
L oveable
L ovely
E xcited
N ice.

Flo-Ellen Britcliffe (6)
All Souls' CE Primary School, Folkestone

My First Acrostic - Eastern England

Kye

K ind
Y ellow hair
E xcellent.

Kye Johnson
All Souls' CE Primary School, Folkestone

Betty

B eautiful
E xcellent
T otally good
T otally funny
Y es!

Betty Appleton (6)
All Souls' CE Primary School, Folkestone

My First Acrostic - Eastern England

Katie

K ind
A nd
T all
I nteresting
E xcellent girl.

Katie Angus (5)
All Souls' CE Primary School, Folkestone

Hangchhu Rai

H elpful
A lways kind
N ice
G orgeous
C areful
H appy
H ard-working
U nique

R eally sweet
A nd friendly
I nteresting.

Hangchhu Rai (7)
All Souls' CE Primary School, Folkestone

My First Acrostic - Eastern England

Ashiph

A good boy
S hort hair
H e thinks well
I nterested in work
P olite and great worker
H andsome.

Ashiph Rai (7)
All Souls' CE Primary School, Folkestone

Jade McClure

J ade has beautiful blonde hair
A sweet heart
D arling
E ver so funny

M arvellous
C uddly
C areful
L ovely heart earrings
U nique
R eally nice
E xcellent.

Jade McClure (7)
All Souls' CE Primary School, Folkestone

My First Acrostic - Eastern England

Star Foss

S pecial
T hankful
A nd I like
R unning

F unny
O h lovely
S oft
S uper.

Star Nicole Foss (6)
All Souls' CE Primary School, Folkestone

Erin Johnson

E rin is funny
R emembers to do her homework
I n time for school
N ice and caring to others

J olly all of the time
O ut of control
H ungry all of the time
N ever angry
S o good at making friends
O utstanding results
N ever nasty.

Erin Johnson (7)
Broad Oak Community Primary School, Heathfield

My First Acrostic - Eastern England

Georgia

G ood
E xcellent
O ranges
R eads
G orgeous
I ntelligent
A ctive.

Mia Terry (6)
Broad Oak Community Primary School, Heathfield

Cookie

C uddly pet
O nly small
O nly fluffy
K ind rabbit
I nteresting
E xciting.

Zoe Thompson (7)
Broad Oak Community Primary School, Heathfield

My First Acrostic - Eastern England

My Poem

J olly James French.
A nice name.
M ake me happy.
E very day I look nice.
S ometimes I am happy.

F resh breath.
R emember to do chores.
E ven does hard work.
N ever is bad.
C ares for his mum.
H ope I get a treat.

James French (7)
Broad Oak Community Primary School, Heathfield

Playing On My DS

L ike playing on my DS

A nd I don't want to get off my DS

R un up the hill

A nd I don't want to stop playing on the DS!

Lara Hands (7)
Broad Oak Community Primary School, Heathfield

My First Acrostic - Eastern England

This Is Ewan

E wan is excited right now.
W ombats annoy me.
A lways silly.
N ever good at home.

H P sauce burns my tongue.
A crocodile man until 5 o'clock.
Z ip destroyer.
E nglish man.
L imper.
T rouble.
I am a human.
N ot an idiot.
E nd of information!

Ewan Hazeltine (7)
Broad Oak Community Primary School, Heathfield

DS Lite

B en likes his DS so much.
E very day Ben plays his DS.
N ever stops playing his DS.

W hen does Ben stop playing his DS?
O oh my DS is white.
O oh my DS is a DS Lite.
D o I have a DS?
T he DS is my best toy.
H orses I ride.
O oh my DS I got when there was only white and black.
R eally like my DS.
P eople like DS.
E asy DS is.

Ben Woodthorpe (7)
Broad Oak Community Primary School, Heathfield

My First Acrostic - Eastern England

Me And My Sister

K ind to people
A ngry at me when I annoy her
T eases me
H ungry all the time
E xcited when dinner is ready
R eally funny to me
I n a temper when my dad shouts at her
N ever lonely
E xhausted when she runs.

Jessica Porter (7)
Broad Oak Community Primary School, Heathfield

Hannah

H ungry all the time
A t school on time
N eat all the time
N ot bad at school
A hungry person
H appy girl

M ad as a hatter
E ats a lot
P eople's friend
H appy, funny girl
A girl who is good
M e, not a boy, I am a girl.

Hannah Mepham (7)
Broad Oak Community Primary School, Heathfield

My First Acrostic - Eastern England

Kieran

K ind to everyone
I s a twin
E xcited at school
R uns in the playground
A rranged to play with my friends
N ot a girl.

Kieran Hands (7)
Broad Oak Community Primary School, Heathfield

My First Acrostic

C allum's hair is blonde
A t football I like drinking
L ikes many things
L ikes football
U nder my bed I keep a football
M y eyes are blue.

Callum Dobson (6)
Copford CE Primary School, Colchester

My First Acrostic

D olphins are my favourite animal.
A t the swimming pool I like going under the water.
I like going to Beavers on Friday.
S cience is my favourite subject.
Y vonne is my favourite name.

N elly, my teddy, is cuddly.
O utside in the garden I like playing with Zoë.
R osie is my best friend.
T ag team is my favourite game.
O ver the holidays I like being with my family.
N umeracy is my worst subject.

Daisy Norton (7)
Copford CE Primary School, Colchester

My First Acrostic

Manchester United fan.
I'm a big brother.
Tigers are my favourite.
Cute is how I would describe my brother.
Ham is my favourite food.
At the zoo I like walking around.
My mum is very nice.

Mitcham Brand (7)
Copford CE Primary School, Colchester

My First Acrostic

L illy likes polar bears,
I like to dance,
L oves chocolate and sweets,
L illy is a good swimmer,
Y o-yos I am not good at!

Lilly Hanson (7)
Copford CE Primary School, Colchester

My First Acrostic

A lice supports Manchester United.

L oves lollipops.

I go to karate.

C urly hair.

E llena is my friend.

Alice Gladwell (7)
Copford CE Primary School, Colchester

My First Acrostic

R osie's eyes are blue.
O liver is my favourite cousin.
S cience is my favourite thing to do.
I go to Brownies on Wednesday with Amber.
E xcellent.

Rosie Fulford (7)
Copford CE Primary School, Colchester

My First Acrostic

Harriet likes African elephants.
All my family are very special to me.
Red is not a very nice colour for me.
Reading is fun to me.
I like to ride my bike.
Eating is one of my favourite things.
Toast and jam is my favourite breakfast.

Harriet Chamberlaine (7)
Copford CE Primary School, Colchester

My First Acrostic - Eastern England

Mummy

Dear Mummy,

Happy Mother's Day,

Marvellous Mummy,
Understands how to play bandits!
Makes good flapjacks,
Magnificent stories,
Yummy cupcakes.

Love from

Mia xxxxx.

Mia Brimilcombe-Cowie (7)
Firle CE Primary School, Lewes

Mummy

Dear Mum,

Happy Mother's Day

M usical
U nderstanding
M arvellous
M agnificent
Y ou are magical.

Love from

David xxxooo.

David Cooper (7)
Firle CE Primary School, Lewes

My First Acrostic - Eastern England

Mummy

Dear Mummy,

M ummy is kind,
U nderstanding,
M arvellous,
M iracles,
Y ou lovely Mummy.

Love from

Madi xxxxx.

Madison Piper (6)
Firle CE Primary School, Lewes

Mummy

Dear Mummy,

M ummy
U nderstanding
M agical to me
M agnificent
Y ou're the best

xoxoxo.

James Pratley (6)
Firle CE Primary School, Lewes

My First Acrostic - Eastern England

Mummy

Dear Mummy,

M arried to Malcolm
U nderstanding
M ummy is cute
M ummy is lovely
Y ummy and fun.

From Nathan.

Nathan Lewis (6)
Firle CE Primary School, Lewes

Mummy

Dear Mummy,

Happy Mother's Day,

My marvellous Mummy,
Understanding me when I want a biscuit,
Makes really nice cakes,
Mummy I love you,
You are the best mummy who has lived.

Love from

Izzy xxxooo.

Izzy Abey (6)
Firle CE Primary School, Lewes

My First Acrostic - Eastern England

Mummy

Dear Mummy,

Happy Mother's Day,

M ummy is married,

U nderstanding,

M agnificent,

M arvellous,

Y ou're the best in the universe.

Love from

Ava xxxxx.

Ava Brimilcombe-Cowie (7)
Firle CE Primary School, Lewes

Mummy

Dear Mummy,

I wish you a very Happy Mother's Day

    M ummy, I love you
    U are marvellous
    M ummy, I love you
    M ummy, you are marvellous
    Y ou are the best.

Love from

Robert xxxooo.

Robert Pratley (6)
Firle CE Primary School, Lewes

My First Acrostic - Eastern England

Mummy

Dear Mummy,

M ummy is cute like a rose
U nderstanding
M ummy
M ummy, I love you
Y ou are nice.

Love from
Luke xxxxx.

Luke Freeman (7)
Firle CE Primary School, Lewes

My Acrostic Poem

J oyful
E xciting
S pecial
S uccessful
I ntelligent
C aring
A mazing.

Jessica Whitehall (7)
Kettlefields Primary School, Newmarket

My Acrostic Poem

Super
Talkative
Excellent
Pretty
Helpful
Active
Nice
Interesting
Energetic.

Stephanie Warr (7)
Kettlefields Primary School, Newmarket

My Acrostic Poem

C heating all the time
H ilarious
A ccuracy - always correct
R eviving
L ively
I ntelligent
E xtreme.

Charlie Nicholas (6)
Kettlefields Primary School, Newmarket

My First Acrostic - Eastern England

My Acrostic Poem

A ctive person
M arvellous girl
Y oung and pretty

S weet lady
E merald Amy
L earning, lively
L ovely lady
E njoying games
R espectful girl
S uper smiley.

Amy Sellers (7)
Kettlefields Primary School, Newmarket

My Acrostic Poem

G ood

E xcellent

O bedient

R ich

G lorious

E xcited.

George O'Shea (7)
Kettlefields Primary School, Newmarket

My First Acrostic - Eastern England

My Acrostic Poem

M arvellous
I ntelligent
L ovely
L oopy
A mazing.

Milla Jarman-Howe (6)
Kettlefields Primary School, Newmarket

My Acrostic Poem

J oyful
A rtistic
M arvellous
E legant
S illy.

James Dracup (6)
Kettlefields Primary School, Newmarket

My First Acrostic - Eastern England

Ellie

E ggs is what my family call me.
L aughs a lot.
L ong hair.
I ncredible face.
E veryone likes Ellie.

Ellie Savidge (6)
Leybourne CE Primary School, West Malling

Freddie

F unny
R ed is my favourite colour
E xtra fast
D oing the right thing
D ancer
I ncredible
E ats a lot of chocolate.

Freddie Francis (6)
Leybourne CE Primary School, West Malling

My First Acrostic - Eastern England

Philip

P hilip is itchy today
H e's a bossy boots
I am seven years old
L ikes 'Guitar Hero'
I know my two times table
P erfectly good.

Philip Coussey (7)
Leybourne CE Primary School, West Malling

Rhiannon

R eally polite

H appy

I ncredibly silly

A good girl

N ice

N early 8 years old

O range is my favourite colour

N ot a nasty girl.

Rhiannon Russell (7)
Leybourne CE Primary School, West Malling

My First Acrostic - Eastern England

Nathan Fox

N osy
A good boy
T ickly
H istory teller
A thletic
N ot naughty

F unny
O dd
X tra good.

Nathan Fox (6)
Leybourne CE Primary School, West Malling

Molly

M olly is beautiful
O h, so noisy
L ovely girl
L ight skin
Y es, we like her.

Molly Booker (6)
Leybourne CE Primary School, West Malling

My First Acrostic - Eastern England

Victoria

Very fine
Incredible at playing hide-and-seek
Clever
Tall
Ordinary
Relaxing
Incredibly funny
Always thinking about when Jesus died on the cross.

Victoria Fleming (7)
Leybourne CE Primary School, West Malling

Michael

Miserable

Incredible

Cool all the time

Hot as well!

Agreeable all the time

Ears are quite small

Listening well everywhere.

Michael Middleton (7)
Leybourne CE Primary School, West Malling

My First Acrostic - Eastern England

Jack

J olly good fun
A crobatically strong
C razily funny
K iss my mum a lot.

Jack Daniel (7)
Leybourne CE Primary School, West Malling

India

I ncredibly cheeky
N ice and helpful
D isabled but very happy
I ncredibly kind
A good girl.

India Fricker (6)
Leybourne CE Primary School, West Malling

My First Acrostic - Eastern England

Easter

E aster egg
A nimals being born
S pringtime is here
T ime to relax and remember Jesus
E veryone enjoys Easter
R isen from the dead.

Hannah Collier (6)
Leybourne CE Primary School, West Malling

Easter

E ggs being eaten
A big event
S end cards to your family
T oo much chocolate
E xciting time for people
R isen from the dead.

Ben Young (6)
Leybourne CE Primary School, West Malling

My First Acrostic - Eastern England

Samuel

S ometimes funny
A ccurate
M athematical
U sually good
E xtra fast
L iteracy mad.

Samuel Dascalescu (7)
Leybourne CE Primary School, West Malling

Alex Kitchener

A rtist
L oving
E xtra fast
X cellent!

K een
I ntelligent
T all
C lever
H airy!
E nergetic
N egative
E ating greedily
R elaxing.

Alex Kitchener (7)
Leybourne CE Primary School, West Malling

My First Acrostic - Eastern England

Kiran

K ind
I ntelligent
R eally fast
A good boy
N ice.

Kiran Henry (6)
Leybourne CE Primary School, West Malling

Nicole

N eat
I nteresting
C lever
O rganised
L ovely
E xcellent.

Nicole Egen (6)
Leybourne CE Primary School, West Malling

My First Acrostic - Eastern England

Amy

A good girl
M arvellous
Y ou always say yes!

Amy Mitchell (6)
Leybourne CE Primary School, West Malling

Jack

J olly
A good boy
C lever
K ind.

Jack Whybrow (6)
Leybourne CE Primary School, West Malling

My First Acrostic - Eastern England

Oliver

O rganised
L ovely
I ncredible
V ery good at sums
E xcellent
R eally fantastic.

Oliver Temp (6)
Leybourne CE Primary School, West Malling

Jarvis

J olly
A rtist
R eally good at writing
V ery good at phonics
I ncredible
S ensible.

Jarvis Spratt (6)
Leybourne CE Primary School, West Malling

My First Acrostic - Eastern England

Phoebe

P retty Phoebe is always
H appy and feels
O K
E very day she is
B est friends with
E verybody.

Phoebe Margetson (6)
Little Snoring Primary School, Fakenham

Liberty

L ovely
I nteresting
B eautiful
E xcellent
R ight-handed
T all
Y ellow hair.

Liberty Cann (6)
Little Snoring Primary School, Fakenham

My First Acrostic - Eastern England

Milly

M illy
I nteresting
L ovely
L ittle
Y ummy.

Milly Eckett (5)
Little Snoring Primary School, Fakenham

Abigail

A bigail's
B est friend
I s Phoebe
G reat games they
A lways play and
I nclude others
L ucy and Milly.

Abigail Cator (6)
Little Snoring Primary School, Fakenham

My First Acrostic - Eastern England

Jurassic Park

J ust got eaten
U p
R oar
A ttack
S care
S cary
I ncredible
C arnivores.

Kyle Williamson (6)
Little Snoring Primary School, Fakenham

Alex

A mazing Alex
L oves to play
E xcellent games like
X -Men and Wolverine.

Alexander Thomas (7)
Little Snoring Primary School, Fakenham

My First Acrostic - Eastern England

My Cat Holly

H appy and
O ld cat. Sometimes
L icking me. Likes
L ovely treats and purrs.
Y ummy.

Kyle Taylor (7)
Little Snoring Primary School, Fakenham

Lovely Gwendolen

G wendolen is

W onderful and

E xciting, smiley all the time

N ice, beautiful and happy

D elicious, she's kind

O bservant, sparkly

L ovely, good and

E xcited about

N eedlework.

Gwendolen Otte (6)
Little Snoring Primary School, Fakenham

My First Acrostic - Eastern England

Flower

F lowers are always
L ovely and sometimes flowers are
O range. Some flowers are
W onderful and look
E xciting and have
R oots that go deep underground.

Daniel Ellis-Flinders (7)
Little Snoring Primary School, Fakenham

Harriet

H arriet
A mazing
R eally
I nteresting
E xciting
T winkly.

Harriet Borley (5)
Little Snoring Primary School, Fakenham

My First Acrostic - Eastern England

Garden

G rowing
A pples
R ed
D elicious
E xcellent
N ectar.

Cazy-Rose Flinders (6)
Little Snoring Primary School, Fakenham

Sparkly Sophie

S parkly Sophie

O bservant

P retty, smart and very

H appy, in fact

I 'm . . .

E xcellent.

Sophie Grinnell (6)
Little Snoring Primary School, Fakenham

My First Acrostic - Eastern England

James

J am is yummy.
A pples are my favourite fruit.
M y auntie is funny.
E paulette sharks are really good.
S ome sharks are good.

James Goodchild (6)
Meridan Primary School, Comberton

Phoebe

P illows are cuddly.

H ershey is Maddie's dog and he is very cute.

O ctopuses are my favourite animals.

E ggs I like.

B reakfast is yummy.

E lephants are nice and big.

Phoebe Stearn (6)
Meridan Primary School, Comberton

My First Acrostic - Eastern England

Liam

L icks lollies
I like cats
A t bedtime I have a cat on my lap
M y grandad is funny.

Liam Cox (6)
Meridan Primary School, Comberton

Jack

J am is tasty
A mbrose is my friend
C akes for tea
K ites can fly.

Jack Jacklin (7)
Meridan Primary School, Comberton

My First Acrostic - Eastern England

Mia

M y friend is called Mini Mia.
I had two dogs called Tuppy and Zoe.
A pples are good because they keep me healthy.

Mia Hoover-Harrison (6)
Meridan Primary School, Comberton

Callan

Cows are my favourite animal
And I like ice cream
Like playing it
Like cake
And blue is my favourite colour
Nettles are bad.

Callan Chambers (5)
Meridan Primary School, Comberton

My First Acrostic - Eastern England

Michael

M y favourite animal is a dog
I am going to get a guinea pig
C astles are old
H obbies are fun
A ll my toys are fab
E lephants are funny
L ollies are really good.

Michael Wilkinson (6)
Meridan Primary School, Comberton

Friends

F riends are very important
R iding our bikes together
I n the park playing together
E yes staring at new things
N ever forgotten
D itches always being played in
S urrounded by fun.

Phoebe Cornell (7)
Meridan Primary School, Comberton

My First Acrostic - Eastern England

Hannah

H appy all the time
A nd she likes fajitas
N aughty but nice
N ervous on stage
A nd Hannah is my best friend
H elpful Hannah!

Yasmin Girling (5)
Meridan Primary School, Comberton

Cat In The Garden

C ats crawling up my legs
A garden full of flowers
T alk nice to the flowers.

Lauren Davy (6)
Meridan Primary School, Comberton

My First Acrostic - Eastern England

Garden

G reen grass grows tall.
A nts crawl up my legs.
R oses smell sweet.
D ens in the trees.
E arth worms wiggle.
N ettles sting my arms.

Madeleine McNiven (6)
Meridan Primary School, Comberton

Springtime

S unshine gleaming in the sky.
P ond with tadpoles swimming fast, fast.
R abbit running faster than me.
I n springtime baby lambs are born.
G rass so green.
T he garden is the best place to be.
I can see bees buzzing everywhere.
M ay is nearly here, everyone cheer.
E verything growing around me.

Mae Bicheno (5)
Meridan Primary School, Comberton

My First Acrostic - Eastern England

Garden

G reen is the grass in my garden.
A nts build houses in my grass.
R oses are my favourite flower.
D eer play at the end of my garden.
E veryone enjoys the garden.
N ever get bored of being outside!

Jacob Sewell (6)
Meridan Primary School, Comberton

Giraffes

G ardens are the wrong place for giraffes.
I magine a giraffe at school like me and you.
R oaming is what giraffes like to do.
A giraffe has brown and yellow spots too.
F licking tongues reach into the sky high.
F riendly giraffes you can feed at the zoo.
E normous giraffes are tall as trees.
S ee the giraffes swaying in the breeze.

Cara Chivers (6)
Meridan Primary School, Comberton

My First Acrostic - Eastern England

Fairies

F luttering fairies like to sparkle.
A mber is the name of the orange fairy.
I have a favourite fairy.
R uby the red fairy is her name.
I love fairies.
E very one of them has a colour.
S affron is the name of the yellow fairy.

Katie Hartwright (6)
Meridan Primary School, Comberton

Rosie

R ocking and dancing is fun.
O ctopus is my favourite thing.
S he doesn't like olives.
I gloo is what I want to live in.
E lephants are my favourite animal.

Rosanna Poll (6)
Meridan Primary School, Comberton

My First Acrostic - Eastern England

Sports

S occer sports
P remier League
O lympic games
R ugby match
T rampolining is fun
S ometimes challenging.

Oliver Payne (7)
Meridan Primary School, Comberton

Chocolate

C hocolate comes in different shapes and sizes
H as wrappers on it
O n my face you will see it around my mouth
C an sometimes have caramel in it
O range flavoured chocolate is my favourite
L ovely chocolate, lovely
A nd it is always very, very yummy
T eeth can sometimes get bad when you have a lot of it
E ating chocolate gives you high sugar levels.

Chelsie Alderman (7)
Meridan Primary School, Comberton

My First Acrostic - Eastern England

Summer

S ummer sunshine
U nder the big umbrella.
M um has made ice lollies
M mmmmm . . . yum
E veryone laughing at . . .
R uby-red lips.

Holly Jones (6)
Meridan Primary School, Comberton

Simpkin (My Cat)

S uper soft
I 'm cute
M ice are nice
P ounces
K itten-like
I 'm soft
N ice rest.

Ellen Gourley (6)
Meridan Primary School, Comberton

My First Acrostic - Eastern England

Birthday

B ring special presents.
I t's an exciting day.
R eady for a party.
T ake a few friends.
H ave a wonderful day.
D oing lots of games.
A lways sing happy birthday.
Y ummy birthday cake.

Leanora O'Mullane (7)
Meridan Primary School, Comberton

Tadpoles

T adpoles turn into slimy frogs - eugh!
A tadpole likes to swim a lot!
D addy frog jumps onto a mummy frog's back to make more frogspawn.
P retty soon the frogspawn will be a rectangular shape.
O n the side of the new round head will grow arms.
L egs grow next!
E very spring more frogspawn is made.
S ummer is here, now the pond will be clear!

Alice Heydinger (7)
Meridan Primary School, Comberton

My First Acrostic - Eastern England

Norwich City FC

N oisy crowds
O n the ball City
R unning with the ball
W in, Norwich, win!
I n the goal!
C heering on
H ot dogs to eat.

C rowd on their feet
I have fun
T ake a penalty
Y es we scored!

F inal score 2-0
C ome on you Yellows!

Sam Collison (7)
Meridan Primary School, Comberton

Cambridge

C lever forever
A cademics made here
M eeting friends
B ridge of Sighs
R oyal history
I n my mind
D iddy dogs
G iving things
E ducation every effort.

Delilah Halpin (7)
Meridan Primary School, Comberton

My First Acrostic - Eastern England

Me

H enry is hilarious
E ven when he's sad
N ever really naughty
R arely ever bad
Y et often rather mad!

Henry Legood (7)
Meridan Primary School, Comberton

Dog

Dogs dig underground to find juicy bones

Owen is a dog's name

Good dogs get a doggie biscuit.

Keenan Christ (7)
Meridan Primary School, Comberton

My First Acrostic - Eastern England

My Very Good Teacher

M y very good teacher, so kind and good
R eading and maths, science too
S itting in a chair marking our work

T eaches us all, no matter what
A nd look over there, here she comes
I gnores, no way she would never do that!
T o me you're fabulous.

Alice O'Connell (7)
Meridan Primary School, Comberton

Ice Cream

I ce
C old
E ating

C one
R aspberry flavour
E xciting
A lways delicious
M elting.

Lucy Carlton (7)
Meridan Primary School, Comberton

My First Acrostic - Eastern England

Eeyore

E very evening
E ndless cuddles
Y ou're grey and floppy
O ld bow in your tail
R eally warm
E eyore, my cuddly toy.

Rebecca Allard (6)
Meridan Primary School, Comberton

Jack

J olly good boy I am
A pples I like to eat
C olouring is great fun
K icking a football with Dad.

Jack Street
Nightingale First School, Taverham

My First Acrostic - Eastern England

Hannah

H ow very cheeky can I be
A bit of a monkey
N ow I'm a pickle
N ot very attractive manners
A n impossible girl
H annah is 6 years old.

Hannah Morris-Jones (6)
Nightingale First School, Taverham

Max

M aking models from Lego
A lways happy and laughing
X mas is a time for giving and sharing.

Max Kelly (6)
Nightingale First School, Taverham

My First Acrostic - Eastern England

Lilli

L illi is my name.
I have long hair.
L ovely light brown is the colour.
L adybirds are my favourite.
I have blue eyes.

Lilli Forster (5)
Nightingale First School, Taverham

Jessica

Just as I was eating my wrap my tooth fell out.

Excellent reader.

Singing is great for me.

Seven is the number I like the most.

I have a little brother called Samuel, I play with him.

Colouring is fun for me

And I love drawing, it makes me happy.

Jessica Williams
Nightingale First School, Taverham

My First Acrostic - Eastern England

Ellen

E llen is six years old.
L ikes to read books and draw pictures.
L aughing and having fun is what I enjoy most.
E nergetic Ellen likes riding her bike with Daddy.
N ice and kind to her baby brother Daniel.

Ellen De-Abreu (6)
Nightingale First School, Taverham

Lauren

L ovely Lauren has pretty eyes.
A t night I dream of beautiful fairies.
U seful at keeping my bedroom tidy.
R eading with my mum makes me happy.
E xcited because I like swimming at school.
N ever ever naughty, always good.

Lauren Mason (6)
Nightingale First School, Taverham

My First Acrostic - Eastern England

Jamie

J amie loves to run.
A lways on the go.
M aking things.
I s always happy.
E ats sweets.

Jamie Fox (5)
Nightingale First School, Taverham

Ellie

E llie is 5
L ovely reader
L oves playing
I ntelligent and bright
E llie loves helping her teacher.

Ellie Vicary (5)
Nightingale First School, Taverham

My First Acrostic - Eastern England

Macy

M oody Mace went to bed late.
A lways playing teachers in her spare time.
C onsiderate, kind, helpful and friendly.
Y ellow and green is the colour of her football team.

Macy Guyton (5)
Nightingale First School, Taverham

Molly

M y name is Molly
O ranges are my favourite fruit
L earning is my favourite thing to do
L emons taste sour
Y orkshire puddings don't.

Molly McCarthy (5)
Nightingale First School, Taverham

My First Acrostic - Eastern England

James

J ames George Nottingham is
A lways thinking about cars
M y hair is black
E yes are brown, and I am
S ix years old.

James Nottingham (6)
Nightingale First School, Taverham

Jordan

J ordan likes jelly
O n the tree I climb high
R eally good to my friends
D on't like nuts
A lways playing with Power Rangers
N ever naughty.

Jordan Barton (6)
Nightingale First School, Taverham

My First Acrostic - Eastern England

Adam

A dam is 6
D oes not like nuts
A ctive all the time
M y toys are special to me.

Adam Cann (6)
Nightingale First School, Taverham

Joshua

J oshua likes to play his guitar
O ften likes to ride his bike
S unny days are the best
H aving fun is all I want to do
U ncovering stones is fun
A cat is my favourite pet.

Joshua Rendlesome (6)
Nightingale First School, Taverham

My First Acrostic - Eastern England

Alana Boyd

A fter school I play tennis.
L ove my mummy
A pples are yummy
N anny gave me a toy
A lana likes helping Mummy

B asketball is lots of fun
O ctopuses have 8 legs
Y ellow walls in my kitchen
D addy loves everyone.

Alana Boyd (6)
Nightingale First School, Taverham

Lucy

L ong yellow hair.

U nder 5 foot tall.

C hocolate is one of my favourite snacks.

Y ellow is one of my favourite colours.

Lucy Nudds (6)
Nightingale First School, Taverham

My First Acrostic - Eastern England

Ebony

E ats sausage and chips
B aby brother is fun
O n the weekend I play babies with my pram
N aughty Ebony always eats food
Y ellow is my favourite colour.

Ebony Leggett (5)
Nightingale First School, Taverham

Yasmine

Y ellow is my colour
A mazing smile
S wimming is fun
M essy me
I like monkeys
N an is the best
E aster eggs I love to eat.

Yasmine Lowe (5)
Nightingale First School, Taverham

My First Acrostic - Eastern England

Lewis

L ewis is very sneaky
E very day he plays on his PSP
W hen it's night
I love to run very fast
S ometimes I'm not good.

Lewis Ricketts (6)
Rainham Village Primary School, Rainham

Paige Blackmore

P aige is a funny girl
A nd she likes to keep secrets.
I like to eat fish and chips.
G oes to the park
E very day.

B e kind to people.
L ikes playing games.
A round her friends.
C an do cartwheels.
K icks a football.
M akes her friends laugh.
O n the trampoline.
R uns quite slowly.
E llie is her friend.

Paige Blackmore (7)
Rainham Village Primary School, Rainham

My First Acrostic - Eastern England

Mollie

M ollie moves around
O n the grass I play
L ike to play with my brother
L ove playing
I love to watch films
E specially with friends.

Mollie Fell (7)
Rainham Village Primary School, Rainham

Lakhan Sunder

L akhan is very good
A ll the time
K ind too!
H e is very smart
A ll the time
N ever eats his dinner

S o I'll give you a hand
U and me are friends together
N ever ties his shoes
'D o them up,' Mum says
E very day!
R eally that's true!

Lakhan Sunder
Rainham Village Primary School, Rainham

My First Acrostic - Eastern England

Rianna Theresa Kelly

R ianna is smart.
I am good at things.
A unty Sandra is great.
N early clever at maths.
N ever good at doing shoes.
A round the class I help people.

T he playground is big.
H er armpit, it hurts right now.
E very day I get stickers.
R ianna loves to eat chips.
E very week I am good.
S kates on her roller skates.
A round the house I help my family.

K icks her football.
E llie is my best friend.
L isa is my mum's name.
L illy is my best friend.
Y o-yos are my favourite toys.

Rianna Theresa Kelly
Rainham Village Primary School, Rainham

Jamie Godson

J amie zooms around

A nd likes apples

M y brain is really good

I like cake

E very day

G ets lots of stickers

O n his jumper

D oes silly things

S o does his brother

O n the beds

N o one tells him off.

Jamie Godson (7)
Rainham Village Primary School, Rainham

My First Acrostic - Eastern England

Niha Raju

N iha is kind
I s very happy
H as lots of friends
A lways has neat writing

R eally helpful
A lways concentrates
J umps on trampolines
U ses a skipping rope.

Niha Raju
Rainham Village Primary School, Rainham

Fidel Joseph

F idel is Rhys' friend
I n the school
D inner is fun
E very day
L oves to laugh

J okes to tell
O nly funny ones today
S ees his friends
E very day
P laying
H appy all day.

Fidel Joseph
Rainham Village Primary School, Rainham

My First Acrostic - Eastern England

Stephen Crews

S miley and happy
T his is Stephen
E very day
P lays with friends
H e likes football
E very day
N ice boy

C upcake
R uns really fast
E very day he plays football
W alks slowly
S lowing down.

Stephen Crews (7)
Rainham Village Primary School, Rainham

Rhys Rose

R hys is Fidel's friend
H e is always happy
Y ellow is not his favourite colour
S ometimes he feels sick

R uns really fast
O n the grass
S o do I
E very day.

Rhys Rose (7)
Rainham Village Primary School, Rainham

My First Acrostic - Eastern England

Connor Clifford

C onnor's very cheeky at home
O n the computer all the time
N ever comes off
N ever great at maths
O n his PS3 a lot
R uns very fast in races

C ollects Ben 10 toys
L ikes 'Little Big Planet'
I love my mum very much
F riendly
F idgets at home
O nline, offline
R uns faster than lions
D oes his work.

Connor Clifford (7)
Rainham Village Primary School, Rainham

Aminatu Belo-Osagie

A lways does hard work
M akes a great carrot cake
I s kind to other people
N ever gets told off
A lways makes people happy
T akes people to the office when people are hurt
U ses capital letters and full stops

B elieves in children
E ats apples
L ikes riding her bike
O rganises the trays

-

O pens the door
S urprises people
A lways plays with people
G ives her brother toys
I s helpful
E njoys playing.

Aminatu Belo-Osagie (6)
Rainham Village Primary School, Rainham

My First Acrostic - Eastern England

Shantae Marson

S hares her sweets
H ates hats
A lways plays
N ever looks messy
T alks too much
A cts well
E ats roast dinners

M akes music
A bides by the rules
R eads well
S ings songs
O beys the rules
N ibbles nuts.

Shantae Marson
Rainham Village Primary School, Rainham

Joshua Alaka

J okes around
O wns a DS
S tays at home
H elps children do their work
U nderstands English
A round people laughing

A nd why do you not do your work?
L ikes girls
A lso I like the sun
K iss girls
A round people.

Joshua Alaka (7)
Rainham Village Primary School, Rainham

My First Acrostic - Eastern England

Dilanas B

D oes make pancakes
I s kind
L ikes pineapple juice
A lways plays Ben 10 game
N ever had a Vilgax toy
A lways plays Yu-Gi-Oh game
S pends time making pancakes.

Dilanas Bidva (6)
Rainham Village Primary School, Rainham

Julia Muja

Julia jumps through hoops
Usually uses an umbrella
Loves lollies
Is good at listening
Always has breakfast

Makes fairy cakes
Understands Albanian
Jogs in the park
Allows her friends to play.

Julia Muja
Rainham Village Primary School, Rainham

My First Acrostic - Eastern England

Katie

K eeps her toys in a box
A sks for sweeties
T akes her teddy to bed
I s always quiet
E njoys her dinner.

Katie Reid (5)
Rainham Village Primary School, Rainham

Camron Brown

C olours nicely,
A cts silly,
M akes chocolate cakes,
R epeats words,
O pens the door,
N ever says, 'No,'

B orrows her mum's bracelets,
R ows with her brother,
O wns her own house,
W ishes her brother wouldn't hit her,
N ike trainers are her favourite.

Camron Brown (6)
Rainham Village Primary School, Rainham

My First Acrostic - Eastern England

Coral Finch

C olours pictures
O pens the windows
R uns around the playground
A lways has a learning body
L ikes skipping

F inds friends helpful
I s pretty
N ever naughty
C hats to her friends
H ates hamsters.

Coral Finch
Rainham Village Primary School, Rainham

Ellie Smith

E ats anything,
L oves her family and friends,
L ikes to take her dog out for a walk with her mum,
I play on my bike,
E njoys learning,

S miles sometimes,
M akes her dad laugh,
I s kind in school,
T akes turns,
H elpful to her friends.

Ellie Smith
Rainham Village Primary School, Rainham

My First Acrostic - Eastern England

Lucy

L ittle girl
U mbrellas are colourful
C ats are cute
Y ellow chicks at Easter.

Lucy Norman (5)
Rainham Village Primary School, Rainham

Max Patrick

M ax is fabulous
A nd he is great
X -ray my finger

P ancakes are good for you
A nd they are lovely
T o run
R un up the hill
I nk is for printing
C ome up the hill
K ick a football.

Max Patrick
Rainham Village Primary School, Rainham

My First Acrostic - Eastern England

Ciaran

C iaran loves his mummy
I play with Oliver
A pples are juicy and sweet
R ed and lovely
A lways see my mum
N ever saw anybody.

Ciaran Robinson (5)
Rainham Village Primary School, Rainham

Kadi Bayliss

K adi is nice

A lways

D ogs are nice

I love my sister

B abies are sweet

A pples are nice

Y ellow is my favourite colour

L ondon is where I live sometimes

I s my name Kadi? Yes

S nakes are my favourite

S lime is not nice.

Kadi Bayliss (5)
Rainham Village Primary School, Rainham

My First Acrostic - Eastern England

Esther

E verybody loves Esther.
S ister has a horse.
T oo much you are eating.
H orses are lovely.
E at, eat a lot.
R un, run, it's time to go.

Esther Showeminio (6)
Rainham Village Primary School, Rainham

Lilian

L ily likes work.

I never get told off.

L et people come to my party.

I write important things at school

A nd always share.

N ever get cross.

Lilian Phillips (5)
Rainham Village Primary School, Rainham

My First Acrostic - Eastern England

Katie

K atie loves everybody
A nd runs about
T o the park we go
I like my sandwiches
E aster eggs are yummy.

Katie Fuller (6)
Rainham Village Primary School, Rainham

Fricis

F ighting is bad
R ead books
I n my house it is nice
C heating is bad
I n my house it is fresh
S ausages are fat.

Fricis Cirulis (6)
Rainham Village Primary School, Rainham

My First Acrostic - Eastern England

Dylan

D ylan eats lots of chocolate
Y uck, I hate fruit
L ambs love to eat grass
A nts like to live underground
N obody.

Dylan Phillips (6)
Rainham Village Primary School, Rainham

Demi

D emi likes chocolate.
E verybody likes eating food.
M yself, I am good.
I nside out.

Demi Daniel (6)
Rainham Village Primary School, Rainham

My First Acrostic - Eastern England

Dillon

D irty Dillon likes mud
I n the house
L ove my mum
L ove my dad
O n the hill
N ice, not!

Dillon Edwards (5)
Rainham Village Primary School, Rainham

Gabby

G o out.
A n ant.
B y myself.
B eautiful beach.
Y ummy fish fingers.

Gabrielle Hartman (6)
Rainham Village Primary School, Rainham

My First Acrostic - Eastern England

Peter

P eter is nice
E aster fun
T o go to the park
E aster eggs are not good for you
R abbits are cute.

Peter Wilson (6)
Rainham Village Primary School, Rainham

Holidays

H olidays are really fun!
O ff I go to watch films!
L ots of people love their birthdays and Christmas.
I love summer days because it's my birthday.
D ays are nice sometimes.
A n apple a day keeps the doctor away.
Y ou know blossom is really pretty on trees.
S ome days are fun and others aren't.

Holly Todd (6)
St Faith's School, Cambridge

My First Acrostic - Eastern England

Bunny

B unny gave me lots of Easter eggs
U nder my dad's favourite flowers
N ormally my bunnies run away and Emily helps me catch them!
N ow they don't run away as much
Y ou would love them!

Sophie Hart (7)
St Faith's School, Cambridge

Day Out

D ad, Hannah, Mum and William
A way to a fun park
Y ummy chocolate

O utside having fun
U p a lamp post
T hen time to go home.

William Best (7)
St Faith's School, Cambridge

My First Acrostic - Eastern England

Easter Egg

E ggs are nice
A nd eat all of them
S tuff yourself full to the brim
E at all you can
R ub your tummy

E ggs are gone
G ive some to another person
G obbling is finished now.

Alfie Godsal (7)
St Faith's School, Cambridge

Skiing

S kiing is fun
K icking the snow is fun!
I like the crunchy ice
I like to kick the ice!
N ormally I fall over!
G reat effort by me!

Hugo Fung (6)
St Faith's School, Cambridge

My First Acrostic - Eastern England

Wild

W hite hot sun!
I love the red squirrels!
L lamas are good but
D ucks are the best!

Emily Townsend (7)
St Faith's School, Cambridge

Gecko

Geckos are harmless and like light.
Eat mosquitoes, geckos do.
Can you catch mosquitoes too?
Keep putting on mosquito spray.
Only problem is, there are no Easter eggs in Mauritius!

Lara Iqbal Gilling (7)
St Faith's School, Cambridge

My First Acrostic - Eastern England

Easter

E aster bunny went to sea
A sunny day for its tea
S melly things make it mean
T iny plants make it eat
E very day I'll do some tea
R eally, what a clever bunny he is!

Rocco Benedetto Mozo (7)
St Faith's School, Cambridge

Brilliant

B uild a tent with Rosie.

R un really fast round the garden.

I n the tent me and Rosie ate

L unch.

L oved the sandwiches!

I like Easter egg hunts

A lways fun!

N ot really big Easter eggs

T asty Easter eggs.

Molly Punshon (6)
St Faith's School, Cambridge

My First Acrostic - Eastern England

Woburn

When I get to see animals
Oh I love the snow tigers!
But I hate the animals that bite
Eureka! I found the snow tigers
Really like the rabbits
Now it's time to go home.

Gavin Watt (6)
St Faith's School, Cambridge

Dreamcatcher

D reaming nicely in your sleep.

R esting in your bed.

E very thought is in your head.

A nd lots of counting sheep.

M ummy is in my dreams beside me.

C hocolate makes my dreams so sweet.

A ny day or night.

T o wake me in the morning.

C aring Mummy gives me a shove.

'H ello,' Mummy says.

E very day she gives me love.

R emember to put your clothes on before you come down.

Edward Ruff (7)
Sproughton Primary School, Ipswich

My First Acrostic - Eastern England

Dreamcatcher

D aylight fades
R ivers glowing
E vening time comes upon us
A nimal dreams fill my head
M aking me toss and turn
C an you help take my dreams
A ll the badness away?
T ill morning comes
C are for me
H elp me sleep through the night
E agle feathers dripping
R unning down, down, down.

Daisy Brosnan (5)
Sproughton Primary School, Ipswich

Dreamcatcher

D reamcatcher, dreamcatcher, catch my nasty dreams
R ustle them far away
E very night I go to sleep
A web up above my head
M y bad dreams fade away
C ome and let the good dreams in
A lways having good dreams
T ill I wake again each day
C almly now I sleep
H our after hour
E ventually I wake up
R eady for a bright new day.

Abigail Thomas (5)
Sproughton Primary School, Ipswich

My First Acrostic - Eastern England

Dreamcatcher

D own I go to my bed
R eally it's quite warm
E veryone gets a kiss goodnight
A m feeling really tired
M y toys are all by my side
C arefully placed
A t last I'm ready to go to sleep
T hinking of playing with Mummy
C aitlin and Daddy too
H aving a really good time
E xploring things to do
R eally it's exciting to have the dreams I have.

Adam Hardy (7)
Sproughton Primary School, Ipswich

Dreamcatcher

D ay becomes night
R eady to sleep
E yes can close
A lways the sun goes down
M aking dream time
C atches the bad dreams
A nd makes them float
T o the floor
C arried on feathers
H appy dreams
E nter my head
R elax and rest.

Ben Marriott-Gregg (7)
Sproughton Primary School, Ipswich

My First Acrostic - Eastern England

Dreamcatcher

D angling beads above my head
R ound and round it spins
E agle feathers smooth and proud
A ll held by golden pins
M agic of the dreamcatcher
C asts its spell around
A t night I close my eyes
T o know that all is safe and sound
C atch those dreams, good and bad
H elp my dreams to keep
E ver watching dreamcatcher
R evolve, I'm fast asleep.

Ellisa Kingham (7)
Sproughton Primary School, Ipswich

Dreamcatcher

D angling down
R ound as a biscuit
E very bead is beautiful
A fternoon sun
M aking it pretty
C atching bad dreams
A fter we sleep
T urning in the wind
C lever web catching
H orrible dreams
E ach morning feeling
R eady for the day.

Mackenzie Cobb (7)
Sproughton Primary School, Ipswich

My First Acrostic - Eastern England

Dreamcatcher

D readful dreams soak down
R acing heart
E ars pound
A ngry thoughts
M onsters frightening
C ruel creatures
A gony
T hunder and lightning . . .
C atch the bad dreams
H elp me please!
E verything's fine
R est at last.

Matthew Earey (7)
Sproughton Primary School, Ipswich

Bananas

B ananas are squidgy
A nother one to eat
N ow I would like another one please
A yellow banana
N ever eat them if they're not ripe
A banana is curved.

Ryan Hard (5)
Whitton CP School, Ipswich

My First Acrostic - Eastern England

Strawberries

S trawberries are juicy
T aste them today
R ipe and tasty
A treat to eat
W ith sugar and cream
B right and mushy
E at them every day
R ed and shiny
R eady in summer
I like them
E asy to pick
S trawberries are healthy.

Aimee Emmerson (6)
Whitton CP School, Ipswich

Grapes

G reen and shiny

R ound and shiny

A nice snack for you and me

P ut them in your lunch box

E at them slowly

S weet and munchy.

Amy Perkins (5)
Whitton CP School, Ipswich

My First Acrostic - Eastern England

Pineapple

P ineapples are juicy
I like them
N ice and sweet
E at them 5 a day
A real treat to eat
P ick them every day
P rickly to touch
L ovely to eat
E at them every day.

Damla Ayran (5)
Whitton CP School, Ipswich

Pears

P ears are crunchy
E at one a day
A pear is juicy
R ipe and yellow
S weet and yummy.

Freddie Acott (6)
Whitton CP School, Ipswich

My First Acrostic - Eastern England

Plums

P ick them when ripe.
L ook at them grow.
U pon the tree.
M um, I found a plum tree.
S hiny purple plums.

Unique Smith (6)
Whitton CP School, Ipswich

Young Writers Information

We hope you have enjoyed reading this book - and that you will continue to enjoy it in the coming years.

If you like reading and writing poetry drop us a line, or give us a call, and we'll send you a free information pack.

Alternatively if you would like to order further copies of this book or any of our other titles, then please give us a call or log onto our website at www.youngwriters.co.uk.

Young Writers Information
Remus House
Coltsfoot Drive
Peterborough
PE2 9JX
(01733) 890066